READY, SET, DRAW!

INSECTS
YOU CAN DRAW

Nicole Brecke
Patricia M. Stockland

M Millbrook Press / Minneapolis

The images in this book are used with the permission of: © iStockphoto.com/Dzianis Miraniuk, p. 4;
© iStockphoto.com, pp. 4, 5; © iStockphoto.com/JR Trice, p. 5; © iStockphoto.com/Boris Yankov, p. 5;
© iStockphoto.com/Anders Aagesen, p. 7; © iStockphoto.com/Maria Toutoudaki, p. 9; © iStockphoto.
com/Péter Mács, p. 11; © iStockphoto.com/Michal Krakowiak, p. 15; © iStockphoto.com/Татьяна
Яковлева, p. 19; © iStockphoto.com/Lisa Thornberg, p. 23; © iStockphoto.com/Lynn Watson, p. 27;
© iStockphoto.com/Nicolas Loran, p. 31.

Front cover: © iStockphoto.com/Maria Toutoudaki (tablecloth); © iStockphoto.com/Lisa Thornberg
(flowers); © Michaela Stejskalova/Shutterstock Images (hand).

Edited by Mari Kesselring
Researched by Emily Temple

Text and illustrations copyright © 2010 by Lerner Publishing Group, Inc.

Millbrook Press
A division of Lerner Publishing Group, Inc.
241 First Avenue North
Minneapolis, MN 55401 U.S.A.

Website address: www.lernerbooks.com

Library of Congress Cataloging-in-Publication Data

Brecke, Nicole.
    Insects you can draw / by Nicole Brecke and Patricia M. Stockland ; illustrated by
Nicole Brecke.
        p.   cm. — (Ready, set, draw!)
    Includes index.
    ISBN: 978-0-7613-4170-3 (lib. bdg. : alk. paper)
    1. Insects in art—Juvenile literature. 2. Drawing—Technique—Juvenile literature.
I. Stockland, Patricia M. II. Title.
NC783.B74 2010
743.6'57—dc22   2009031966

Manufactured in the United States of America
1 – BP – 12/15/2009

TABLE OF CONTENTS

ABOUT THIS BOOK

Honeybees, ants, and dragonflies! Find out what the buzz is all about. With the help of this book, you can begin creating your own fun bugs. Make a monarch butterfly. Or draw a praying mantis. Soon you'll know how to make many different insects.

Follow these steps to create each insect. Each drawing begins with a basic form. The form is made up of a line and a shape or two. These lines and shapes will help you make your drawing the correct size.

A First, read all the steps and look at the pictures. Then use a pencil to lightly draw the line and shapes shown in RED. You will erase these lines later.

B Next, draw the lines shown in BLUE.

C Keep going! Once you have completed a step, the color of the line changes to BLACK. Follow the BLUE line until you're done.

WHAT YOU WILL NEED

PENCIL SHARPENER

COLORED PENCILS

HELPFUL HINTS

Be creative. Use your imagination. Read about Madagascar hissing cockroaches, grasshoppers, and Goliath beetles. Then follow the steps to sketch your own amazing insects.

Practice drawing different lines and shapes. All your drawings will start with these.

ERASER

Use very light pencil lines when you are drawing.

Helpful tips and hints will offer you good ideas on making the most of your sketch.

PENCIL

Colors are exciting. Try to use a variety of shades. This will add value, or depth, to your finished drawings.

PAPER

Keep practicing, and have fun!

HOW TO DRAW A MADAGASCAR HISSING COCKROACH

These shiny brown insects can make a big fuss.
When male Madagascar hissing cockroaches fight, they often hiss loudly at each other. The battling bugs also use their large horns during combat to knock each other around. Only the males have horns. These cockroaches find food on the forest floors of Madagascar, an island east of Africa. The bugs eat plant materials and fruit. Female Madagascar hissing cockroaches carry their young in an egg case inside their bodies until the offspring are big enough to be born alive.

1 Lightly draw a base oval and center baseline. Add a rounded triangle with a bumpy line on one side.

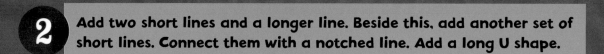

2 Add two short lines and a longer line. Beside this, add another set of short lines. Connect them with a notched line. Add a long U shape.

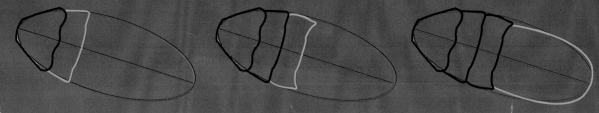

3

Make a pair of short, bent lines on each side of the head. Draw a longer, curving pair on each side of the next section. Add the last pair of legs to the top of the U shape.

4

Carefully erase your baseline and shape. Add two antennae, a small horseshoe shape, and a row of dots.

5 Now it's time to color your Madagascar hissing cockroach!

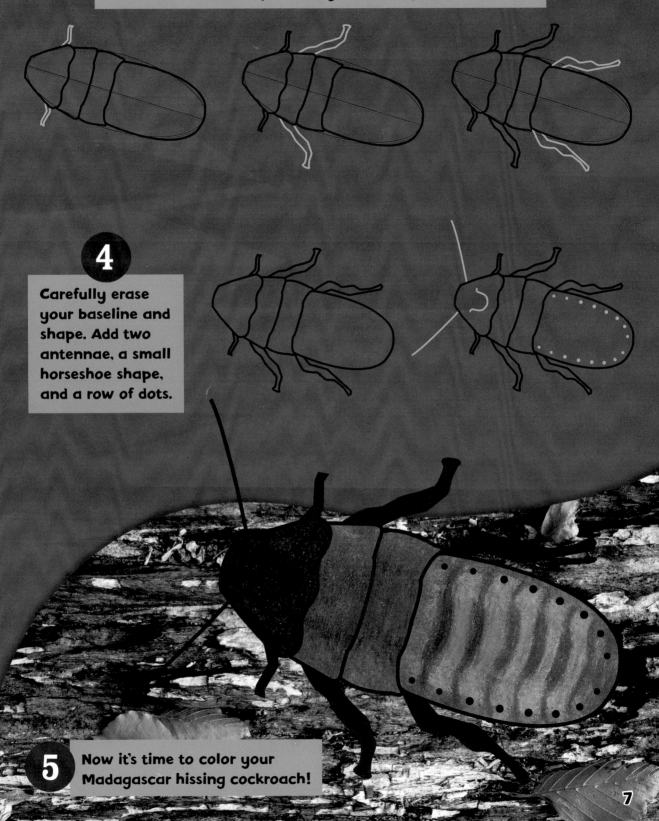

HOW TO DRAW AN ANT

The ever-busy ant is a tough bug. These insects have a segmented body and hard exoskeleton. This acts like a shell for the ant, keeping its insides safe. Ants live in colonies with many other ants. Within a colony, ants are divided into three classes, or levels: workers, queens, and males. Every ant has a job in its colony! Workers feed and protect the queen and her larvae, or offspring. The queen is in charge of the colony. Male ants mate with queens to produce the colony's eggs. Depending on their species, queens can live from a few years to more than forty years.

1 Draw a small base oval and a slightly curved baseline. Use the base oval to draw the head. Add a curved, notched line behind the head. Make another line that looks like a stretched out W.

2

Draw the back. Connect a pair of long, zigzagging lines to make the first leg. Make the next leg.

3

Use two pairs of long, pointed lines for two more legs. Add two short, curved lines. Make the remaining two legs.

4 Erase your baseline and shape. Add a bent antenna, a cupped mouth, and an eye.

5 Now it's time to color your ant!

9

HOW TO DRAW A GOLIATH BEETLE

Goliath beetles are friends to the planet. These African insects feed on ripe fruits and decaying plant matter, helping to keep Earth clean. Goliath beetles are also striking for their size. These bugs get big! A Goliath beetle can reach 5 inches (13 centimeters) in length and weigh 3.5 ounces (100 grams). Ridges on the front legs help these beetles climb trees and dig into the soil. Goliath beetles have hard exoskeletons, oval-shaped bodies, and antennae on their heads. Look for interesting markings on their bodies!

1 Draw a base oval, center baseline, and smaller base oval. Use the smaller base oval to make the head.

2 Add a rough oval shape behind the head. Make a pair of flattened ovals on the back.

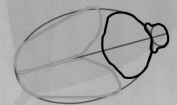

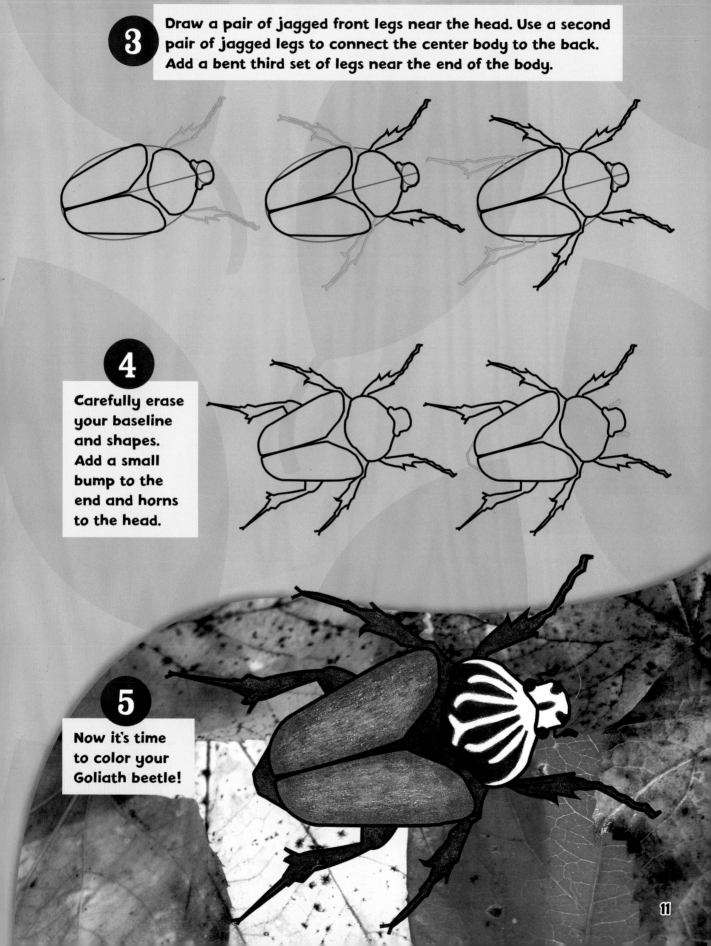

3 Draw a pair of jagged front legs near the head. Use a second pair of jagged legs to connect the center body to the back. Add a bent third set of legs near the end of the body.

4 Carefully erase your baseline and shapes. Add a small bump to the end and horns to the head.

5 Now it's time to color your Goliath beetle!

11

HOW TO DRAW A GRASSHOPPER

The grasshopper gets its name from its jumping skills. This strong-legged creature can hop high and far. A grasshopper can also fly short distances, thanks to a pair of wings. These insects are quite large. Some species can be as long as 5 inches (13 cm). Grasshoppers are also known to cause trouble in fields. Some types will damage crops by eating large amounts of the plants. You may have seen green or brown grasshoppers, but the bugs can be different colors too, including yellow or red.

1 Draw a long base oval. Add a baseline above it. Make a small base circle at one end.

2 Draw a pointed oval for the head. Add an eye. Draw two long antennae. Make a cape shape behind the head and a short line under the chin.

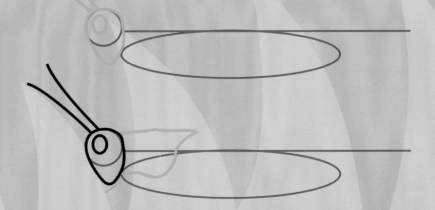

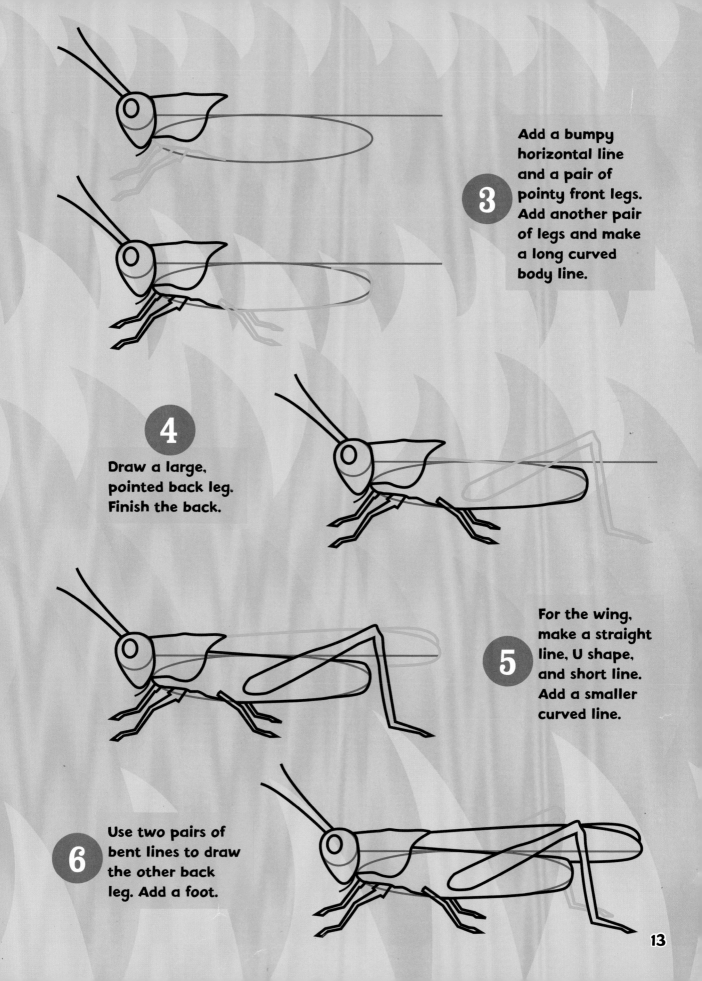

3 Add a bumpy horizontal line and a pair of pointy front legs. Add another pair of legs and make a long curved body line.

4 Draw a large, pointed back leg. Finish the back.

5 For the wing, make a straight line, U shape, and short line. Add a smaller curved line.

6 Use two pairs of bent lines to draw the other back leg. Add a foot.

7 Carefully erase your base shapes and baseline.

8 Draw curving lines and small dots along the body.

EAT YOUR GREENS

Most grasshoppers are herbivores and love to munch on plants.

DRAW A JUICY LEAF!

A

B

C

Some species of grasshoppers change colors as the seasons change.

9 Now it's time to color your grasshopper!

HOW TO DRAW A
HONEYBEE

Do you know where sweet, tasty honey comes from? Ask a honeybee! These hardworking insects live together in beehives. Inside a beehive are wax honeycombs, which are made by worker bees. Similar to ants, honeybee colonies also have workers, males, and queens. Worker honeybees collect food for the queen and build the wax honeycombs. Male honeybees are called drones. Their job is to mate with the colony's queen to produce eggs. The queen bee lays eggs. The worker bees will do a sort of dance to tell other bees where to find food. They collect this food in their honeycombs.

1 Draw a baseline and a small base oval. Add an overlapping base circle. Add a larger overlapping base oval. Outline the head and two eyes on the small base oval.

2 Make a curved line near the neck and add two curved triangles for wings. Finish outlining the body.

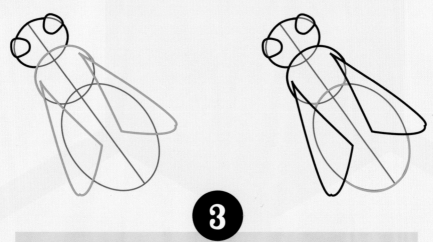

3

Draw a set of straight legs near the head. Add a pair of longer, bent legs to the outside of the wings.

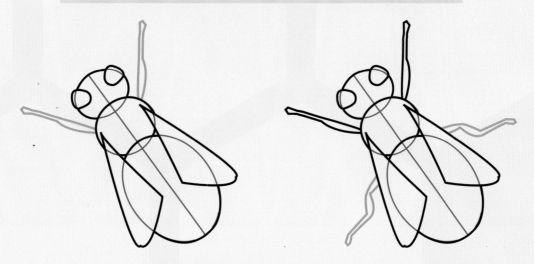

Fast Fact...
HONEYBEES HELP POLLINATE MANY TYPES OF PLANTS.

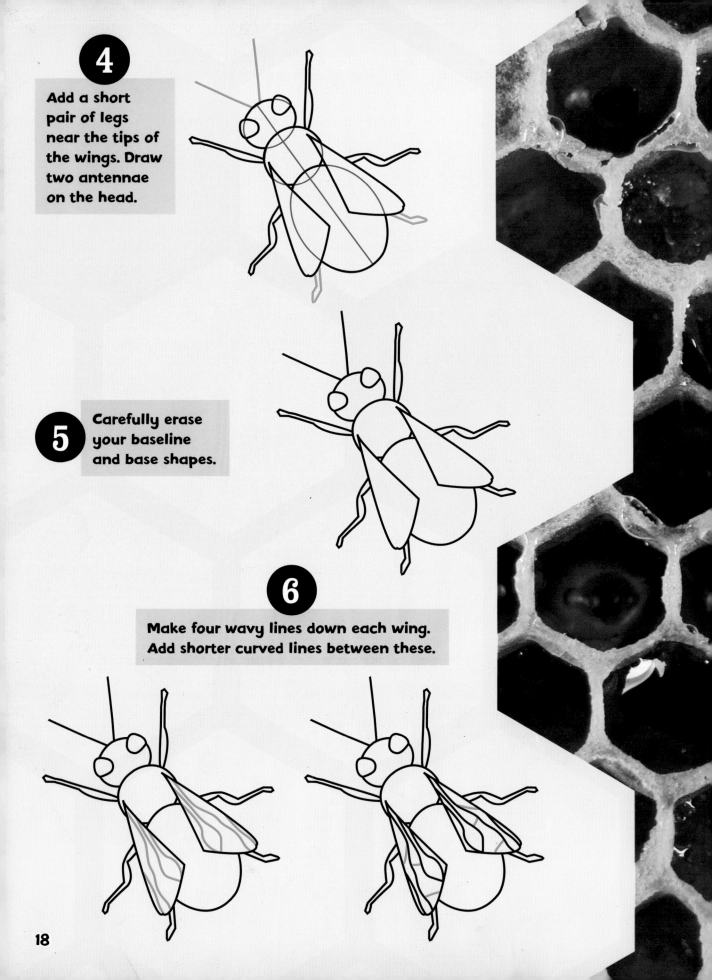

4

Add a short pair of legs near the tips of the wings. Draw two antennae on the head.

5 Carefully erase your baseline and base shapes.

6

Make four wavy lines down each wing. Add shorter curved lines between these.

18

Honeybees must live together in colonies to survive.

7 Now it's time to color your honeybee!

TRY THIS
Use short strokes to show hair.

19

HOW TO DRAW A MONARCH BUTTERFLY

What is that delicate bug fluttering by? It might be a Monarch butterfly. These insects are famous for their long flights. Each winter, groups of monarchs will migrate (move from one area to another) from the northern United States to Mexico and Southern California. Some of the butterflies travel nearly 2,000 miles (3,219 kilometers). The colorful black, orange, and white wings of the monarch warn predators to stay away. These butterflies taste bad. In fact, they're poisonous. Monarch butterflies usually live for six to eight months—a short life for such long flights!

1 Draw a very small base circle and a baseline. Add a large base oval. Make a bumpy **C** shape around the base circle.

2

Connect the C shape's tips with a bumpy line. Draw a fan shape around the base oval. Add a curved bumpy line inside the edge. Make a fin shape above this and another bumpy line inside the edge.

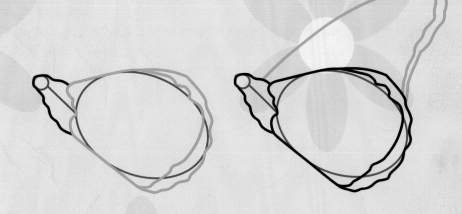

3 Add two bent antennae to the head. Make a short, bent line. Draw four legs, two with wider tops.

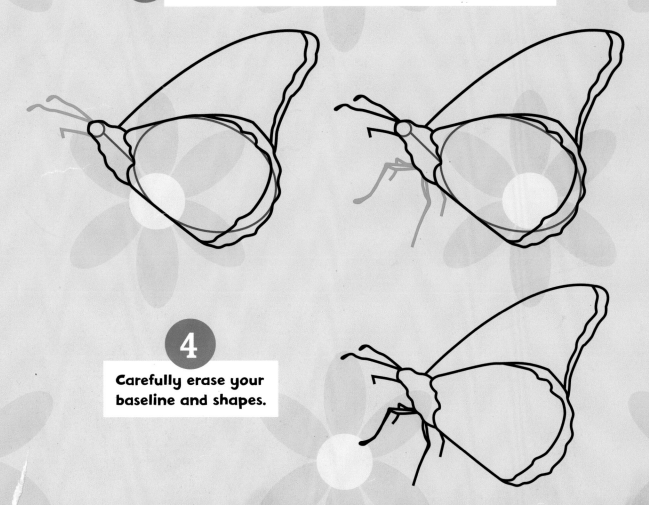

4

Carefully erase your baseline and shapes.

5 Draw four longer shapes in the bottom part of the wing. Add three more shapes. Make three more shapes in the top part of the wing. Add three curved lines.

FLYING FRIEND

Ladybugs are often out and about at the same time as Monarch butterflies.

DRAW A LADYBUG!

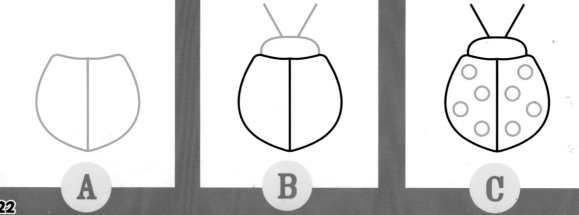

A   B   C

6 Now it's time to color your Monarch butterfly!

A GROUP OF BUTTERFLIES is known as a flutter!

HOW TO DRAW A DRAGONFLY

You can find dragonflies by lakes, rivers, streams, and other freshwater. These helpful insects feed on pesky bugs such as gnats and mosquitoes. A dragonfly has two pairs of wings, which help it fly faster than most other insects. Its legs are designed for grabbing and carrying prey. When the dragonfly flies, it holds its legs in a rounded position. Dragonflies lay their eggs near the water. After dragonfly nymphs, or babies, hatch from their eggs, they move into the water. The nymphs live in the water until they grow wings.

1 Draw a very small base circle and a long baseline. Add two small ovals to the circle. Draw a curved line to connect the ovals.

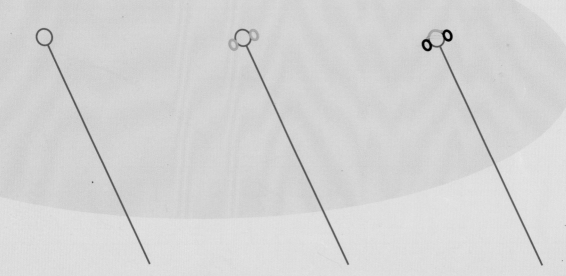

2

Add two parallel curved lines from the head. Draw two long parallel lines with a slight curve at their ends.

3

Use long, pointed ovals for the first pair of wings. Add another set of wings.

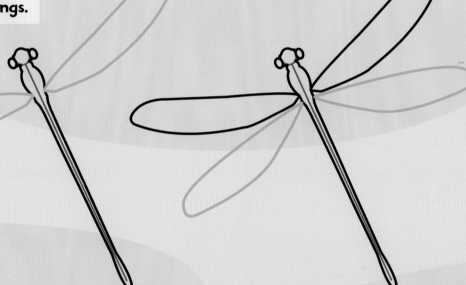

4

Draw an L shape on each side of the body. Add three more short lines to each side to complete the pairs of legs.

5 Carefully erase your baseline and base shape.

6

Make small horizontal lines between the long parallel lines.

Dragonflies live everywhere on Earth except the polar regions.

TRY THIS

Use a little silver and white to add shimmer to the wings.

7 Now it's time to color your dragonfly!

HOW TO DRAW A PRAYING MANTIS

The praying mantis isn't picky about its food. These insects are carnivores, or meateaters. Their prey includes flies, grasshoppers, moths, crickets, and even other praying mantises. The praying mantis uses its long legs to grab food. Spikes on the mantis's legs keep prey from escaping. The praying mantis is shaped like a twig and often brown or green in color. These features help the bug blend in with leafy surroundings. Large eyes on its triangle-shaped head give the insect sharp eyesight. A praying mantis can see motion 60 feet (18 meters) away.

1

Draw a very small base circle and long baseline. Add a small kernel shape to the circle. Make a longer curving line. Add two shorter bent lines.

From the open space, draw two parallel zigzagging lines. Connect the tips with a small Y shape for the first leg. Add another leg. Use a pointy S shape for the next leg.

3 Draw another leg using a connected V shape. Make a bottom leg using two connected Z-shaped lines.

4 Use a long triangle for the back. Add a slightly bent line under this. Draw the other back leg.

5

Carefully erase your base shape and baseline. Add two long antennae and a large eye to the head. Draw a long line along the wing.

MEAL DEAL

Lots of insects feed on flies.
A praying mantis will gobble them up too.

DRAW A FLY!

A

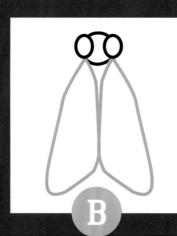

B

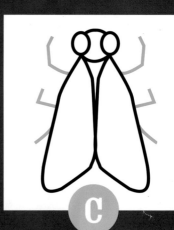

C

LONG AGO, people thought the praying mantis had magical powers.

6 Now it's time to color your praying mantis!

QUICK TIP
Use shading to create depth.

FURTHER READING

Bishop, Nic. *Butterflies and Moths*. New York: Scholastic Nonfiction, 2009.

Glaser, Linda. *Dazzling Dragonflies*. Minneapolis: Millbrook Press, 2008.

Insects and Bug Activities
http://www.dltk-kids.com/Crafts/insects/index.htm

Kalman, Bobbie. *The ABCs of Insects*. New York: Crabtree Publishing, 2009.

Kids and Teachers
http://www.orkin.com/learningcenter/kids_and_teachers_games.aspx

Starke, John. *High Definition 3D: Bugs*. New York: Sterling, 2009.

What Is an Insect?
http://kids.yahoo.com/animals/insects

INDEX